Thank You for purchasing this book!

Welcome to
Dr. Lyn Is In

Practice Angels:
How to Build a Full Private Practice
With Good Referrals Alone

Author, Lyn Kelley, Ph.D., CPC
Certified Professional Coach
"My mission is to empower people to move to the next level of success in their careers."

Practice Angels:
How to Build a Full Practice from
Good Referral Sources Alone

By Lyn Kelley
Published by Lyn Kelley and distributed at
www.Amazon.com

Copyright 2024 Lyn Kelley

I0500987

What others are saying about Dr. Lyn's Books

Hello Lyn, I think you are one of the angels you talked about! I actually feel so motivated that here I am to thank you again. Thank you for your generosity with all the wonderful forms, letters and yourself.
---Elani Aquino, LCSW, Santa Cruz, CA

Lyn Kelly is AISOME. Her ebooks are the books. There are so many garbage marketing books at the bookstore, garbage marketing seminars, people trying to take a lot of money from health care practitioners teaching marketing. Every other book/class is just psycho-babble. Full of stupid tips likes "be positive," "attract clients to yourself," "whatever you do, do consistent."

OK, the psych stuff and being in the correct frame of mind of important. It's not worthless, but to be successful you also need an action plan. You need the right mindset, plus a concrete plan to execute. Lyn Kelley does both! And she has amazing actions plans. The great things is, she has a whole list, full of details on how to execute each one. If one strategy isn't right for you, another one will work. Her ebooks are the absolute best!
---Saul Marcus, Pittsburgh, PA

Thank you so much for your book. You're right, it does work as soon as you use it. Your workbook exercises Ire most helpful. I am already getting positive responses.
---Charie Levy, MFT Brooklyn, NY

Dear Lyn, I found your workshop so inspirational! It has taken me to another level in my consciousness about the work I do as therapists and it has further inspired me to continue my pursuits in

the realm of Organizational Development and Transformation. Your being is quite a catalyst. I appreciate what you are doing very much and feel honored to have been able to experience your work and its profound effect, first-hand.
---Jeanine Gonzalez, Dallas, TX

See more e-Books by Dr. Lyn distributed at
http://www.amazon.com/

I offer telephone and email coaching. Contact me to set up an appointment!

growpublications@yahoo.com

Learn more about Dr. Lyn and Personal and/or Career Coaching at
http://www.growtraininginstitute.com/

Follow me!
FaceBook: http://face-book.com/ lyn.kelley1
X: http://wefollow.com/JanesGoodAdvice
LinkedIn: http://www.linkedin.com/in/drlynisin

Become a Certified Professional Coach (CPC) through
GROW Training Institute, Inc.

The least expensive, quickest and most comprehensive program available! All can be done through Home Study and Online! See Application on our website with all the Most Frequently Asked Questions
www.GrowTrainingInstitute.com

See my YouTube videos:
How to Become a Certified Professional Coach:
http://youtu.be/ZBHrDhxodWc

https://www.youtube.com/watch?v=Ue_2SajS_SY

Practice Angels:
How to Build a Full Private Practice
With
Good Referral Sources Alone
By Lyn Kelley, Ph.D., MFT, CPC

Table of Contents

INTRODUCTION:
The 3 Reasons Referrals are Your Most Cost-Effective Way to Build a Successful Practice
Why You Can't ASK for Referrals
The Simple and Dignified Way to Get More Client Referrals
The Most Essential Components of Success
The One Huge Mistake Clinicians Make that Guarantees Failure
The Value of a Satisfied Client
The Single, Most Important Attitude that Moves You From an Average Provider to a Successful Provider

CHAPTER ONE: You're Only Looking for a Few Good Clients
Learn to Say "No" More than you Say "Yes"
Why You Can't Depend on Long-Term Clients or Client Referrals
The Six Magic Words that Get People to Pay Your Full Fee

CHAPTER TWO: Who Are Your Worst and Best Referral Sources?
Your 6 Worst Referral Sources
Your 10 Best Referral Sources

CHAPTER THREE: How to Get Current and Inactive Clients to Refer to You
The ONLY Way to Get Clients to Refer to You (without asking them to)

The 3 Reasons Clients Leave Treatment Too Soon
The 7 Magic Words that Turn Phone Inquiries into Cash-Paying Appointments

CHAPTER FOUR: How to Create a FREE Monthly Newsletter
The Step-By-Step Plan to Get More Referrals through a FREE Newsletter
Tell, Don't Sell
Write, Write, Write
Coaching Works!

CHAPTER FIVE: How to Get New Referral Sources
The Most Effective Way to Get the RIGHT Professionals to Refer to You
The Magic of Your FREE OFFER

CHAPTER SIX: How to Get Physician Referrals
The ONLY Ways to Get Doctors to Refer to You
What to Give Physicians After a Referral to Ensure They Will Send You More

CHAPTER SEVEN: How to Create Your Own Audio CD's
Why Audio CD's Work in Getting Referrals
Your Simple, Step-by-Step Plan to Create Audio CD's or MP3's

CHAPTER EIGHT: How to Get Referral Sources to Keep Sending You More
Exact Guidelines for How to Thank Your Referrers
Gratitude and the Law of Attraction
What to Send at the Holiday Seasons to Make Your Referrals Skyrocket
The 3 BEST Ways to Thank Referral Sources
A Simple Letter, Sent to the Right People, Done the Right Way Will Swamp You With New, Good Business

Sample Thank You Letter
Sample Coupon that Compels People to Call You

CHAPTER NINE: Why You Should Accept Credit and Debit Cards
Benefits of Hiring a Billing Service
Never Bill Out Again! The 1-2-3 System that Gets 99% of Clients to Pay You at the Time of Service
Get Rid of Your Collection Accounts
It's Actually Quite Easy to Get Paid When You Have Experts Working for You

CHAPTER 10: 10 Simple Things You Need to Do Right Now

CHAPTER 11: The Most Effective Marketing Strategies (Which are not marketing!)
How to Target and Promote SPECIFICALLY to a Well-Pay, Self-Pay Clientele
How to Get People to KNOW-LIKE-TRUST You
How to Obtain Your GOLDMINE List – Your High Yield Target Market

CHAPTER 12: Integrating Social Media
The FREE Online Promotion That Makes You a Celebrity
7 Essential Rules for Building a Loyal Customer Base from Social Media Networking
Social Networking Do's & Don'ts

CHAPTER 13: Dramatic No-Cost Results from YouTube
It's Easy, FREE, and You Can Do It Yourself

BONUS: 7 Ways to Double Your Income Without Advertising or Spending ANY Money

Introduction

The 3 Reasons Referrals are Your Most Cost-Effective Way to Build a Successful Practice

Great News: You can build your entire practice with self-pay clients simply with a few good referral sources! I call them "Practice Angels" because this is what they are for you. While you are working, playing, relaxing or sleeping, your practice angels are flying all around mentioning your good name to their clients/patients/associates. They are your BEST source of good, new clients. Why are they the best? One reason is that it doesn't cost you any money (except for your thank you note and postage stamp). It doesn't cost you very much in time. Another reason is that they are usually professionals who work with many people and therefore can give your name to a lot of people (you need a lot of calls). Another reason is that it is usually a reciprocal relationship wherein you are giving them referrals as well, and you are developing an "affiliation" with this referral source that is mutually beneficial and satisfying.

This book is mainly written for mental health practitioners, life and business coaches, and healthcare providers. Yet the principles apply to almost any profession. However, you need to keep in mind that the human services professions – that is, those professions where you develop an ongoing business relationship with clients – are very unique in the way they should be promoted. You need to get people to "know-like-trust" you. This is important because they will be entering into a relationship with you and they especially need to know they can trust you. One of the best ways to have people trust you right out of the gate is to be referred by someone they know and trust already.

Why You Can't ASK for Referrals

You need to develop and nurture relationships with the right people — people who can help you succeed. Almost everyone you know and meet is a potential referral source. You don't need to "ask" people for referrals, in fact it is unprofessional to do so. You simply need to let people know what you do, give them some business cards and/or information about your practice. If they are in business, offer to exchange business cards and you will refer people to them as well (if appropriate).

You will need to have at least five or six good referral sources. Most healthcare providers I talk to only have one or two good referral sources, yet they know that is not enough! Then they wind up calling me for practice building consultation when things are slow. One or two referral sources simply won't cut the mustard. The reason is that referral sources can come and go like the weather. They may meet a new healthcare provider who they like better, or who is calling them more, or who they want to give a break to. They may send too many managed care clients who cannot or will not pay your full fee. They may move or close their practice. They may get upset if you do not treat every single person they send your way. Then again, they probably have the same slow seasons you do – so when they have fewer clients, you will have fewer clients. You cannot put all your eggs in one or two baskets! I will tell you how to get five or six good referral sources and keep them happy.

The Simple and Dignified Way to Get More Client Referrals

You're also going to learn how to serve your current patients better. When your current clients are happy with your service they will naturally want to refer others to you. You will find that they actually want you to assist them with more conditions than they presented in the beginning. They may not even know consciously that they want assistance in other areas of their life, but a good clinician can feel this out and bring it out in the client. Many times, clients are reluctant to bring up other issues as they don't want you to see them as a problem client or a chronic complainer. There are many ways you can be sensitive to their needs and not appear pushy or "money-grubbing."

There are ways to serve your patients better and actually make more money in the process. Not because your goal is to make money, but simply because you're serving them better. If serving them Ill for their initial presenting problem is worthwhile for them, they will be more apt to return when another problem arises. I will be discussing the concept of "intermittent" treatment (when appropriate), as opposed to time limited treatment with closure and termination.

Of course, you never would try to keep a client in treatment when this does not serve their best interest, only yours. You must keep your ethical integrity at all times. Ethics in marketing the healthcare practice is a topic that is of such great concern that it will be interwoven into every chapter in this book.

You will learn how to generate new referrals and find your best sources for referrals. A referral based practice is a dignified professional method of building a business. There is no greater compliment as a healthcare provider than to receive referrals from a respected colleague or other source.

The Most Essential Components of Success

The following is a list of what I believe to be the most essential components of an effective and successful clinician. Take some time to evaluate yourself as a healthcare provider with regard to each point. If you feel you may be weak in any area, do what you know you should do. Get some additional training in this area, or request assistance from a more experienced colleague. Commit to being the best provider you can possibly be.

Therapeutic Alliance
Unconditional positive regard
Empathy
Good clinical judgment
Ethics and confidentiality
Healthy Boundaries
Effective Diagnosis
Modeling
Coaching
Knowledge of theoretical orientation
Practice within scope of expertise
Effective Interventions
Effective closure and/or termination
Outcomes
Continuing education

Keeping yourself informed is one of the most important aspects of sound private practice effectiveness. There are three most effective ways to stay on top of your profession and take care of yourself professionally. One is to subscribe to a few professional newsletters, journals, or magazines. The second is to belong to your major professional organizations. The third way is to join with a group of trusted colleagues for regular contact for support, supervision, guidance, professional consultation, and/or just communicate with.

The One Huge Mistake Clinicians Make that Guarantee Failure

The one huge mistake clinicians make that virtually guarantee their failure is setting their fees too low. When you lower your fees, you lower your value. People do equate fees with value. Set your fees at least as high as the UCR (usual, customary and reasonable) for your specialty and area.

A healthy, successful clinician knows the value of his/her services, and reflects this with confidence to potential and current clients. She knows there is a market for her -- a segment of their community that values her services. He knows that people will pay for what they value. She knows that people will pay her full cash fee if they perceive her to be an expert who can help them achieve their goals. He knows that in order to reach his market, he needs to follow certain guidelines which are outlined in this book. She knows that in order to create new business, she needs to educate her market about what she does, how she does it, and why it is of value to them. There are no short-cuts.

Who you are is more important than what you do in the treatment room. Clients will sense your enthusiasm for your work, and it will rub off on them. So when you are working in your specialty area with clients who value your work and are motivated to work, you will naturally be more successful!

The Value of a Satisfied Client

It is also important that you find out what the value is of a satisfied client. This will make you look at potential clients much differently. If you do not think you can satisfy a client, it is best to be honest with him/her and refer him/her elsewhere. Not only because that is the ethical thing to do, but it will free up your time and energy to focus more on the clients you can satisfy. You will see why this is a good investment of your time in the long run.

What is the average fee in your practice? Let's say that the average fee is $80 per visit and each client who is satisfied makes an average of 12 visits to you each year. So now you can see that the average annual fee per year, which is 12 times $80, would be $960.

Now, I'm going to assume that the average satisfied client will return to you at least once during the next five years. This would amount to another $960. So two times $960 is $1,920.

Now, the average satisfied client will typically refer at least one new client to you every five years. The satisfied client may refer quite a few other satisfied clients, but for this worksheet, let's just consider that they only refer one person to you over their lifetime. The sum of your original satisfied client, plus the referral together is $3,840.

But remember, this is still only the tip of the iceberg because the person that was referred to you will probably also refer someone else to you. You can build your practice fairly well by client referrals.

For many of us, a large part of our job satisfaction comes from out earnings because earnings are a concrete measure of success. The two aren't always synonymous, however. I all know of those who are financially successful, then fall flat on their faces. But you must believe it is possible to be successful as a healthcare provider and financially successful as well.

The Single, Most Important Attitude that Moves You From an Average Provider to a Successful Provider

The single most important mental health attitude that separates the really successful provider from those who just get by is "possibility thinking." This concept is so extremely valuable if you ever have a chance at thriving in this over-glutted healthcare market. You must believe that you can do it. Then, you must believe that experts can help you. Then, you must be willing to learn, learn, and continue to learn from the experts. These are your role models -- people who have gone before you and paved the way, invented the wheel, learned through trial and error what works and what doesn't work. Learn as much as you can from as many experienced, successful clinicians as you can.

Oprah says you should do what you love. Do who you are. Follow your calling. You must do what you were born to do. When you find your gift, your purpose, your calling, you cannot NOT do that. Even if it doesn't pay huge dividends in monetary terms, you need to do it and keep doing it. You need to keep improving it, and stay with it. Tell everyone who you are and what you do. Get excited about it. Shout it from the rooftops. Dig in your heels, and never, ever give up!

Don't ask yourself what the world needs; ask yourself what makes you come alive. And then go and do that. Because what the world needs is people who have come alive.
---Harold Whitman

CHAPTER ONE:
You're Only Looking for a Few Good Clients

Learn to Say "No" More than you Say "Yes"

I need to tell you something up front. If you do what I say in this book, you will be generating a lot more calls than you could possibly handle. This is GOOD!!! Here's a good lesson for life. You must learn to say "no" more than you say "yes." You simply cannot treat every individual that is referred to you! Do not worry that people won't like you if you say "no." In fact, people trust you even more when you tell them the truth – if you are not the best fit – and refer them to a specialist who could help them. If you do not want to deal with managed care or insurance companies, just be honest and up front about it. Most people will understand, especially when you explain how damaging it could be for them down the road to lose confidentiality.

The best way to be happy as a healthcare provider is to have a full, consistent practice with at least 70% private pay -- full pay, a waiting list with eager potential clients, and a few new potential clients calling you each Week. You need to take care of yourself first, and **think of your business as a business**. Do not worry that if you turn away a client that is referred by a particular referral source, that referral source may not refer to you again. That may be true, but not likely. Since you must keep all information about clients and/or potential clients confidential, you do not need to explain to your referral source why you did or did not accept that client. In fact, you cannot say anything about the client, whether they called or did not call, came in or did not come in, without your client's written

permission. Yes, some referral sources will go astray. This is why you need at least five or six to keep the fires flaming. The best thing you can do is start
NOW to WOO more, good referral sources!

Why You Can't Depend on Long-Term Clients or Client Referrals

Here's the reality. You can no longer depend on long term clients or word of mouth referrals to keep your practice full. People are transient. You MUST have at least five or six good referral sources. You MUST have a steady supply of 2 -3 new potential clients calling you each week in order to keep your practice full. Some of you have said to me, "But Lyn, I can't see that many people!" I tell them "of course not." You are not going to actually SEE 2 – 3 new clients a week! Hopefully, you will see about one new client a Week, and if that's more than you can handle, you will create a waiting list. Some of you have said to me, "But Lyn, is a waiting list ethical?" I tell them of course it is. Those who are in emergency situations you may choose to see right away, or refer them out to a colleague. As soon as you have a waiting list, (good news!) it's time to raise your fees.

Therefore, if 2 – 3 new potential clients are calling each Week, you will probably have to say "NO" to 2 of them. Why? Because they will be asking questions like, "Do you take Cigna?" or "Gee, you're fee is high, can you cut it in half for me?" or "I can only come after 7PM at night due to my husband's job, kid's hectic schedule, etc."

The Six Magic Words that Get People to Pay Your Full Fee

Now, here is where it gets tricky. You need to set your fee and stick with your fee. You need to know you are worthy of that fee. You need to only work with insurance plans that are GOOD for you and PAY WELL. You can choose to see some low-fee and/or no-fee and/or insurance clients, but keep it to a minimum (10-30% of your practice) and only see them during your most open and convenient hours, i.e., 10AM – 3PM M-F. If you ever want to build your practice and your income, you will need to start saying "NO." You can say, "I wish I could, but I can't." Or, "I have a waiting list." Explain why you are worth your fee, explain why you do not take managed care, and inform them of who you are and how you work. Sometimes they will turn around and say, "OKAY."

State your fee matter-of-factly. Say the six magic words. "My fee is $100 per hour." Practice saying this over and over until you're comfortable with it. Once you have stated your fee, BE QUIET!!! Do not say anything silly like, "But, if that's difficult for you, I do have a sliding scale," or "What can you afford?" No other professional does this, why should you??? The ONLY words that should come out of your mouth after you state your fee are, "I do accept all major credit cards." You would be surprised how many people will accept your full fee if you accepted credit cards! If you do not yet accept credit cards, this is the MOST IMPORTANT thing you can do right away! Call your bank or one of the large membership clubs such as Costco on how to accept credit cards the easiest and least expensive way.

You must learn to say "no" to MOST of the potential clients who call you. You are not looking for 30 problematic clients so you can work 60 hours a Week and earn $40K a year! You are looking for a few GOOD clients, so you can see about 25 good clients a Week, work about 30 hours and earn $100K+ a year! A GOOD client is one who pays your full fee at the time of treatment, shows up for their scheduled sessions, and does the work you ask them to do.

How do you create a 'money magnet'? You must overcome your money illusions. One common illusion is that money is limited. Since the universe is literally infinite, with inexhaustible, transformable resources, your financial possibilities are also unlimited. Your immortal self or soul knows this.
--John Demartini

CHAPTER TWO:
Who Are Your Worst and Best Referral Sources?

Your 6 Worst Referral Sources

First I want to tell you where the <u>worst referral sources</u> are. You may have read other marketing books that told you these are great sources of referrals, but all those books are either outdated, or they are adhering to an old fashioned recipe found in the Business Administration archives of some Ivy League college. They simply do not send enough referrals your way to make them worth expending a lot of time, money, and resources on. There are exceptions. You might be the rare and lucky healthcare provider who belongs to several "buddy systems" and your "buddies" send you lots of referrals. But they don't work for the majority of providers.

Colleagues: Sorry, but your professional colleagues who are in private practice just aren't going to refer <u>good</u> clients to you. At least not often enough to warrant you sending them mailers, advertising in your professional association's local chapter newsletters, or trying to wine them and dine them. They need to build their own practices in this over-glutted market. There are a couple of exceptions to this. First, they may send you a lot of managed care, low-fee, or no-fee clients (since they do not want to accept low fees and massive paperwork, and <u>neither do you</u>). Second, they may refer good clients to you if you have a very specialized niche, i.e., children, infertility, gastric bypass surgery, borderline personality disorder, multiple personality disorder, gender identity, gay/lesbian, alternative lifestyles, schizophrenia, and others. If you have a specialty that most other healthcare providers do not have, you would do well letting them know that you have this specialty, as they are always looking for referral sources for clients who have more specialized needs.

Public Schools: Unfortunately, schools have become so concerned about liability that in most districts, they are reluctant or prohibited from referring to any private practitioner. They usually will only refer out to government funded agency personnel, and in many cases, these are the only providers they will even allow to be guest speakers in student classrooms. There is a much more effective referral base within the private schools. To get referrals from private schools, you can either mail the guidance counselor your information followed up with a phone call, or call and ask if you can speak at one of their teachers' meetings or parent/teacher association meetings. The PTA president would be a great referral source for you!

Attorneys: Many lawyers are afraid that a healthcare provider will be another influencing factor in their client's life who may talk them out of the lawyer's advice. They want to maintain control of the client's decisions and situation. They may not trust that a professional such as you could help in a legal matter. Most divorce attorneys do their own mediation. They tend to want to keep their clients "in-house." Attorneys usually do not refer to therapists unless their client is extremely problematic. Again, exceptions to this rule would be if you have a specialty niche that would be of interest to their field.

Mental Health Agencies: If the mental health agency caters to low income clientele due to government subsidies, they will probably send you clients who tend to not be able to pay your cash fee and/or who are problematic.

Crisis Hotlines, Emergency Personnel Directories: I would not recommend that you pay to be on one of these lists, however, if it is free for you, and you don't mind treating some people who are low-pay or no-pay, go ahead. Again, most people who call a hotline or who are referred by emergency personnel tend to <u>not</u> be your self-pay, full-pay type of clients.

Psychiatric Facilities: Hospitals, Day Treatment Centers, Drug/Alcohol Rehabs and Residential Treatment facilities may get clients to call you, but too often they are not successful in showing up for an appointment. Unfortunately, the clients who have been treated in one of these facilities do not generally make the best fee-for-service clients. Cost, location, transportation, lack of social support all make it difficult for them to get in on a regular basis.

Stop wasting time with people and organizations that don't refer to you. Start spending your time more wisely. It's fine to socialize with people who don't send you referrals, but when it comes to business, you must be selective about your time.

Your 10 Best Referral Sources

Your best referral source is your <u>current clients</u>. This is because they already know you and have a good relationship with you. There is a marketing strategy that works well for health care providers. This is: KNOW – LIKE – TRUST. The best referrals come from people who <u>know you, like you, and trust you</u>. Once you get a good referral, it is your job to make sure he/she knows you, likes you and trusts you.

Referral sources depend on you, your location, and your specialties. But those that have proven to be the best are:

Corporations & Large Businesses

Businesses you frequent, i.e., printer, hair stylist, doctor, dentist, waiter/waitress, travel agent, veterinarian, etc.
Alternative Healers (chiropractors, acupuncturists, massage therapists, etc.)
Churches and Synagogues
Special Interest Clubs or Associations (Sierra Club, Gay & Lesbian Associations, Parents without Partners, AAUW, etc.)
Labor Unions, Professional Organizations (PTA, AARP, Women in Business, etc.)
Internet Referral Directories
Chamber of Commerce
Business Associations & Networking Groups
Physicians

Some healthcare providers have asked me if it is beneficial to join a lot of business associations. Unless you have lots of free time and thoroughly enjoy going to meetings, being on committees, doing volunteer work, and supporting the cause, do not waste your time where you will not get a rich source of referrals. Most business associations are not for healthcare providers. You are better off joining the local chapter of your own professional associations. I would definitely recommend attending the local chapter meetings of the American Medical Association, as you will find a rich pool of referrers at these meetings. Also, being on the board of almost any business or professional association will further your positive reputation in your community.

It's not about who you know, it's about who knows YOU.
--Lyn Kelley

CHAPTER THREE:
How to Get Current and Inactive Clients to Refer to You

The ONLY Way to Get Clients to Refer to You (without asking them to)

Again, active and inactive clients give the best referrals. This is one good reason to continually stay in contact with inactive clients. By sending them your newsletters (or other information) on a regular basis, you will be fresh in their mind, should a problem arise with themselves or their friend, co-worker, or relative. Do send a thank you note to the referring client, if your referral client gives you permission. You may have a space on your intake form that asks, "Whom may I thank for referring you?" They sign this form, and then you have permission to send a thank you note to your referring client. A thank you letter is the best way to get your referral source to continue to send you more new clients. This is one way of actively promoting your practice, without even realizing it.

Do not ask current or inactive clients to give you referrals. Do not send them thank you gifts. Just give them a nice thank you note, and that's all. Those of you who have attended my seminars already know about my "tell -- don't sell" philosophy. I live in an information age. People want and need information. They want and need YOUR information. You have "intellectual property" that is extremely valuable to others! The best way to promote your practice is to give away bits of that information for FREE. This is what attracts people to you. They come to get the information, value the information, and appreciate you for giving it to them. They also feel they have gotten to know you better by receiving your information. They begin to connect to you, trust you, and feel good about you. They assume that if they got this information of value, then you must have more of it, and therefore, assume that they will receive more value by entering into coaching or treatment with you.

One of the best, most cost-effective ways to stay in touch with former clients and keep getting new referrals while providing a great service is to send a monthly or bi-monthly newsletter.

3 Reasons Clients Leave Treatment Too Soon

Research shows that 45% of healthcare patients leave treatment too soon. How soon is too soon? Before they have achieved the goal(s) the came to you with. The three main reasons they give for leaving too soon are 1) confused about fees, 2) didn't feel the clinician cared about them, and 3) an attitude of indifference in the provider and/or staff. You can prevent this loss by following these simple steps. First of all, when your client comes in for their first visit, they should always be greeted warmly. They should always be listened to and treated warmly and empathetically.

When clients come in initially, they always have a "presenting problem." Ask your client to write on their intake form the answer to this question. "How will you know when you no longer need the services of a (whatever your specialty is)?" This way, during your first session, you can create goals for your clients. Coaching them along the way, with a step by step plan for achieving their goals, and writing it down for them, will cause them to realize how much you are helping them.

Always give your clients these three things before they leave each visit. These three things will make it much more likely that they will show up for their next scheduled visit and remain in treatment until they are well.

1. An appointment card for their next visit, with your NO-SHOW policy written on it.
2. A homework assignment. This will be something you have created during your session or something for them to do, such as look up information on a website.
3. An affirmation card. Write a positive affirmation for them to keep handy and accessible between visits. Have them read it over every day, at least three times. It's astonishing what a positive impact this will have in their lives – plus it will make it MUCH more likely that they will show up for their next scheduled visit!

The 7 Magic Words that Turn Phone Inquiries into Cash-Paying Appointments

If you follow all my advice in this book, you will be getting way more calls than you could actually take on as clients. Once a prospective client calls, you need to determine if they will be a good, well-paying client. 90% of the time, a good, well-paying client has nothing to do with how much money they make, how much they can afford, or what kind of insurance they have. It completely depends upon their MOTIVATION. So the best way to determine their motivation is to ask a question such as, "What caused you to call a (your specialty) today?" They will then begin to share their story with you and you will be able to sense what their motivational level is.

Don't worry if potential clients keep you on the phone for 20 or 30 minutes. You should be offering a free initial phone consultation anyway, to determine "goodness of fit." The more time you spend with potential clients on the phone before they make an appointment, the more likely they are to make (and keep) and appointment. Not only that, but you will be connecting with people in an important and valuable way. Even if they don't make an appointment now, they may later on. And chances are great that they will speak very highly of you to their friends and family. Creating good relationships with ALL people is the key to building and keeping a successful practice.

Your goal is to motivate your clients to become healthier, happier, and more peaceful. You can reduce their anxiety by reassuring them, validating them, encouraging them and supporting them. Become an expert motivator by reading my book *How to Motivate Your Clients to Change.*

> *Success leaves clues.*
> **---Tony Robbins**

CHAPTER FOUR:
How to Create a FREE Monthly Newsletter

---Nothing happens until something moves.
*---***Albert Einstein**

Tell, Don't Sell

You don't need to be good at advertising, marketing or promoting in order to be successful in business. Your number one, best promotion for the healthcare practice is being a good educator. You need to spend some extra time educating your clients about what is best for their overall health. Take time to ask questions and listen for their answers. Give them empathy and unconditional positive regard. The Oprah show became the number one talk show in the world because she was the first talk show host who asked questions, listened, and gave empathetic feedback. We could all become more successful if we practiced these skills!

If you want to attract new, self pay, full pay clients, and you dislike selling and marketing, then a newsletter is just right for you! You will be promoting yourself and your specialties, and you will be giving something of value. There are numerous advantages to you to doing a newsletter. After I started mine, my coaching and consulting business doubled in the first few months

Other benefits to you:
It's virtually free to you
It can be done from your home computer any time
Helps prospective clients get to know you better and connect and trust you

Enhances your credibility
You get known as an expert
Increases your exposure in your community
Keeps you in continuous contact with your current and former clients
Reminds people to refer to you
Provides excellent information to the community
Provides a public service
Helps build referral sources
More opportunities for speaking engagements and media exposure
Reminds people of ALL your services, i.e., coaching, group treatment, classes, books, etc.
You can submit your newsletters to local newspapers as articles
You give your clients something of value that they appreciate
You get to find out what they want through e-mail feedback
You are helping people more than you realize
You can reach out to people all over the world
You breed familiarity – you get your professional name known
You attract new clients
Current and former clients will send them to their friends and family
You get lots of positive responses
You have written a book within a year (if you write your own)
It's fun!

      There are two ways to do a newsletter. The EASY way or the HARD way. The <u>hard</u> way is to write it yourself (how long have you been saying you'll do it, but don't?). The <u>easy</u> way is to have someone else write it for you and put your name and photo on it. This is similar to having a "ghost writer" like most popular authors do. Then hire a mailing house to get it mailed out, or a web automation service to get it e-mailed out.

Below, I have outlined the two ways to do your newsletter. The first one is the hard way – it is the less expensive, do-it-yourself method and will take about 3 – 15 hours a month of your time. The second one is the easy way because you don't have to write it yourself, but will cost you between 70 cents to a dollar each for hard copies, and less for the online version.

You can't expect to get the jackpot if you don't put a few nickels into the machine.
--Flip Wilson

Here's your step-by-step "Do-it-Yourself" plan:

1. Get as many e-mail addresses as you can. Ask all your current clients, former clients, colleagues and referral sources for their e-mail address. Your e-mail list is like gold to you.

2. Your newsletter should be free, so clients can get a chance to know you and connect with you. It can be monthly or bi-monthly or quarterly.

3. Your newsletter should contain a link to your website (if you have one, and I highly recommend that you do) as Ill as a link to your e-mail address. This way, they can find out more about you and ask you questions and get to know you better.

4. Have a catchy title for your newsletter. Some ideas are "The Connection," "Good News for Creating Fantastic Relationships," "Soar with Your Life," "Live Your Best Life," "The Happiness Factor," etc.

5. Use your newsletter to inform clients and potential clients about any changes in your practice, a new class, workshop or group, new office hours, new locations, new staff, new equipment, etc.

6. Offer a "Tip of the Month" on each of your specialty areas. Or a monthly affirmation. Or a calendar for the month with daily affirmations.

7. Write a short article (no more than one page) about a topic you think would be of interest to them. You can also include a questionnaire, activity or "check-up." People love to take little quizzes and find out more about themselves or their loved ones. Cartoons are also fun (as long as they would not offend anyone). If you have a group practice, ask each colleague to contribute something to the newsletter. If they do, they will get their name in print, as Ill as their photo.

8. Do put your photo in your newsletter. Let people know of anything new in your office, any new training you have received, and any new classes, workshops or groups you may be offering.

9. Ask them what they want! Offer surveys and/or questionnaires to find out what topics are of greatest interest to them. You can also use this as a forum to ask what book titles, class titles, or article titles would be of most interest to them. This way, when you create any form of advertising, you can use the words in your "catchy headline" that get the best response from the most people.

10. Ask your recipients to send your newsletter on to any other interested people. Make sure you also give instructions on how they can be added or removed from your newsletter list. This way, more new potential clients will sign up for your newsletter, and you can bet these new people will be interested!

11. Keep your newsletter professional, short (one to three pages) and general. If they want more in depth information, they can either find it on your Website or call you. Be careful not to be too narrow in focus or opinionated. People shy away from "fanaticism." As difficult as it may be, do not get on a soap box! Stay out of politics. Do not be pushy.

You can tell them about upcoming events in the community, good movies to see or interesting books to read as long as they are on the subject of your professional specialty.

12. Don't give personal information about yourself or your family. You can tell a story about yourself as long as it isn't too personal. Do not discuss clients, even if you leave out their name. Saying things like "I had a client tell me the other day that…" is too much information. That very client may be reading your newsletter and be quite unhappy to hear you have shared what they told you in confidence.

13. Make sure you mention your "FREE Newsletters on all your marketing and promotional materials. Simply state "Sign up for my FREE e-mail newsletter" and provide your e-mail address.

14. Make sure to mention your "FREE Offer" in your newsletter. Your free offer is something of value that you give away to allow people a chance to get to know you better and feel they will benefit from your service. This could be a free first 30-minute phone consultation, a free first assessment session, an expert report, book, CD, pamphlet, etc. Also include a photo of yourself so they can connect with you and remember you.

15. Make sure you send your newsletter out as "blind copy" which means that each recipient will NOT get all the e-mail addresses you've sent the newsletter to. If you need instructions on how to send out "blind copy" you can contact your Internet Service Provider who will walk you through it. It's easy once you get it!

16. You can use any e-mail program to send your newsletter. If you want to get fancy, you can subscribe to an e-mail automation service or a newsletter service which handles all your graphics, photos, logos, text layout, etc. for you. I use www.easywebautomation.com which costs about $50

a month but is very easy to learn. This service automatically sends an e-mail response to anyone who gets added to my e-mail list. This response usually goes something like "Thank you for signing up for my FREE Monthly E-mail Newsletter." I write my newsletter any time during the month, upload it to the service with a scheduled date to be released, and press a button. That's it! If you tell them GROW Training Institute and Lyn Kelley referred you, you will get a discount.

Write, Write, Write!

Each month's newsletter can be an article that you can also submit to local newspapers and magazines for publication, which is another form of free promotion! Remember, each newsletter can be a chapter of your book (that you've been wanting to write for the longest time)! Within a year, you could have written a whole book, or at least an E-book! A book is a great promotional item and you can also earn extra money with a book. As you can see, your newsletter has a SNOWBALL EFFECT!

Coaching Works!

I write a monthly newsletter for Coaches to give their clients & referral sources called *Coaching Works*. It is about two pages, specifically to be emailed and/or added to your website. It takes me about five to ten hours a month to write these newsletters – why waste your time? For about $70 a month you can have it done for you. You put your name on the newsletter – I'm simply your "ghostwriter." See a sample on my website: http://growpublications.com/newsletter/CoachingWorks.html

CHAPTER FIVE:
How to Get New Referral Sources

The Most Effective Way to Get the RIGHT Professionals to Refer to You

To get the right professionals to refer to you, you need to target those who are most likely to refer to your specific specialty. Once you've determined who these professionals are, you'll want to get to know them – or get them to know YOU. The best way to do this is to stop by their office for a visit. Even if you can't meet them on this visit, you'll at least get to meet the office staff and drop off some of your materials. You need to keep sending something to these professionals – something with your name on it – over and over. Studies show it takes an average of nine contacts before someone actually calls. Be persistent.

A great way to get professionals to refer to you is to offer them something of VALUE. Getting referral sources to display your business card or brochure is often a tough sell. What is more sellable is to give them an <u>informative article or your newsletter</u> (either one you've produced, or one you've read and gotten permission to reproduce) with <u>your</u> name and phone number at the bottom, and <u>their</u> logo, name and phone number at the top! You would present the articles to them, asking them to choose which ones they would like to display in their waiting room/office. Then ask for their letterhead stationary, and print the article onto their paper. This way, they get the credit for educating their clients/patients, and you get your name out as an expert/referral source.

This doesn't have to be a major writing project on your part. In fact, you can get articles from professional associations, web sites, and other resources that give permission to reprint and distribute for educational purposes. For example, the American Academy of Child and Adolescent Psychiatry's (AACAP) web site has more than 60 articles that can be reproduced for personal or educational use without permission.

The Magic of Your FREE OFFER

One of the questions asked at my "Promote Your Practice" seminar is, "Is it ethical to give a free 30 minute consultation? Aren't you entering into a therapeutic relationship at this point, and shouldn't you get informed consent first?" As most of you know, I encourage you to offer a <u>FREE 30 minute consultation</u> with new, potential clients, either by phone or in person. The reasons for this are:

1. It helps the client to get to know you and how you work, in order to determine if you would be a good "fit" for them and their problem.
2. It helps you as healthcare provider to get to know the client's problem and determine if you could help them, and if not, refer them to someone who can.
3. It provides an opportunity for you to inform potential clients about who you are, how you work, your theoretical framework, experience, education, training, etc.
4. Potential clients are often quite fearful of their first contact with you. It helps the client to begin to feel they know you, can trust you, and thereby open up to you.
5. It begins the "joining" process, and helps set the stage for a possible therapeutic relationship to develop, if appropriate.
6. Most healthcare providers are already spending at least 30 minutes on the phone with new

potential clients anyway, so why not offer it as a "volunteer service"?

7. It makes it more likely that potential clients will call YOU as opposed to other providers who do not offer this service.

8. Your referral sources will see this as a benefit to them as Ill as their clients/patients.

The reason I believe this offer is ethical is that both you and potential clients have the right to some communication prior to a contractual arrangement for treatment or coaching services, to determine "goodness of fit." This is NOT treatment or coaching time. It is more of a short evaluation period for both parties to see if they can work together. Just about all other professionals (attorneys, CPA's, financial planners, stockbrokers, real estate agents, cosmetologists, specialty physicians, surgeons, etc.) offer this service.

Later, I'll provide you with a "sample coupon" that you can have printed and give to your referrers. Most professionals will display your coupons, especially if it is for a free service. This free offer is not a marketing ploy. It is a way for you to <u>promote yourself and your services in a way that is also educating and helping people to make good decisions for themselves.</u> I have found that every potential client I have provided this service to has greatly appreciated it. If you are not comfortable offering this free initial service, then don't do it! I give you lots of other effective promotional ideas to choose from. You need to choose the ones that work for you and feel right to you. As with the therapeutic relationship, your relationship to your promotions needs to have "goodness of fit" as well!

Realize the power of your word. Your word is the power that you have to create. It is a gift that comes directly from God.
---Don Miguel Ruiz

CHAPTER SIX:
How to Get Physician Referrals

The ONLY Ways to Get Doctors to Refer to You

Physicians can make the best or the worst referrers. I will tell you why they are a difficult source to try to market to, and then I will tell you the only way to successfully get good referrals from doctors.

First of all, most doctors are worried about maintaining their own practices also. They tend to be disease-oriented and operate under the medical model. They are worried that "shrinks" might talk the patient out of the medical advice the doctor gave him/her. They are afraid to refer out because if their patient is not happy with the referral, it is a reflection on the doctor who made the referral, and the patient might find another doctor. Also, if the referral doesn't work out, the doctor may be <u>legally liable</u> (you are at least partially responsible for your referrals). The doctor just doesn't have time (or won't make the time) to get to know you and how you work, and is unlikely to refer to someone he/she doesn't know Ill. Doctors may also fear they will lose points with managed care plans if they refer out too often. Then, there are many doctors who will not even discuss non-medical concerns with patients (some won't even confront a chronic alcoholic!) for fear of losing the patient. The greatest obstacle is that most physicians are members of HMO's, and can only refer out to other providers on the patient's HMO plan.

Here are some ways to get physician referrals, if you don't mind spending time, energy, and money trying to win over this group of referrers. If you win, it's a great referral source. If not, you've wasted your time. I think the potential gain is worth the energy.

Go to the physician's office —
Unannounced, introduce yourself to the receptionist, tell him/her what you do, give him/her your business card & brochure <u>with a gift</u> (discussed later). Then ask the receptionist if you can have a few minutes of the doctor's time, or make an appointment. Usually you will at least get to meet the doctor and have a few words of exchange. If he/she says, "I'm very busy, I'll call you," ask if you can leave some business cards and brochures (and preferably an audio CD for the doctor to listen to on his/her way home from work). Be sure to let them all know that you also are in a position to <u>make</u> referrals. At least you will be able to have the doctor read your literature, and this alone, may work into referrals.

Call Physicians
— Ask your current clients for permission to talk to their physician when there is an overlap with a medial problem. Physicians are usually very supportive of collaboration between professionals and may not talk to you but for this reason. Be sure to get a signed release from your client before you make the call.

Medical Building
— As Donald Trump says, "Location, location, location. Try to locate your office in the same building with as many doctors as possible. Not only do patients like the convenience and comfort of receiving their mental health and physical health care in the same building, but it makes you look more professional and more clinical. The doctor would prefer to refer to a healthcare provider that is close, to make collaboration easier (or seem easier). If the provider isn't close by, he/she will probably go unnoticed by most doctors. You could even ask physicians about the possibility of sharing space, or subleasing space from them, even just for one or two evenings a Week. Most doctors

do not use their offices in the evenings and they might jump at the chance to have the extra income.

Letters to Physicians — This is not as effective as going to visit in person, but it may get you your first connection. Send the doctor a letter introducing yourself. Include any articles, books or CD's you've written or tapes you've produced that would have relevance to the doctor's specialty. Also include a handful of business cards and your "free offer coupons." Your materials will be seen as a bonus to physicians and they will be encouraged to send their patients to a practice that delivers something extra. Call the doctor after a few days and ask if he/she has had a chance to look over your information. Ask him/her for 10 — 15 minutes of their time, so you can come to their office and meet. If they are receptive, bring them something on your visit. It sounds corny, but bringing the office staff a box of candy does go a long way (especially if one of them helped you get the appointment with the doctor!).

Get to Know Their Office Staff — The doctor's staff may be in a good position to make referrals. They can recommend you to the doctor, or to the patients. Take time to visit with them if they are open to it. If they want to tell you about their sister in law's addiction to reptile breeding, listen intently. The office staff is a rich referral source.

Keep in Touch — Keep these doctors on your mailing list. It may be three years down the road that you finally get a referral, but it is worth it. If you are treating one of their patients, be sure to provide timely follow-up information (with patient release). Treatment plans and closing summaries are appreciated and doctors will be amazed that you took the time to write them and send them. Stay fresh in their minds!

Write Thank You Notes — Write thank you notes for everything. Thank the doctor for meeting with you, referring to you, talking with you on the phone, working so Ill with a mutual patient, etc. This is a great way to stay in touch. Have some thank you notes printed up with your name and logo on them, that look professional. You can even have an assistant or secretarial service write the note (you dictate) and mail it for you.

Target Family Practices — Family practice physicians, pediatricians, and general practice are the best doctors to target. Psychiatrists are like your colleagues, preferring to keep as much business as possible in house.

Think Like a Doctor — When doctors make referrals to other doctors, these patients get first priority and first class treatment. If the doctor makes the referral, they usually want you to see their patient right away. See the patient as soon as possible and right after the appointment, send the doctor a thank you note stating you have met with the patient already. The doctor will be impressed.

Go Where Physicians Are — You may not be able to hang out at the golf course, the country club, or the black tie hospital charity functions, but you can attend the meetings that doctors go to. Physicians are required to obtain **CME** credits so go to these meetings. Go to their local AMA chapter conventions and meetings. Go to EAP meetings where providers are invited. In all cases, keep a positive mental attitude. Remember, in this surging managed care market, most physicians are feeling financial cuts and feel they are being devalued. If you let them know you feel the same way, they will want to get to know you better.

Send Gifts at Holidays – Discussed in Chapter 8.

What to Give Physicians After a Referral to Ensure They Will Send You More

I will keep saying it over and over, thanking people goes a long way toward your success in life! When you thank the referrer, you should do so in writing, in your handwriting, on a nice thank you card (preferably with your name and logo on it – get some pre-printed cards that look professional yet nice). Do not send gifts, as this would seem like a payback or a barter, which is unethical. Just send a nice thank you note saying, "Thank you for the referral. It's professionals like you that help make my practice successful." You don't need to write the client's name in the thank you card. The professional will probably know who it is, and even if they don't, it's okay.

When this referral source keeps getting thank you notes from you, they will keep sending you referrals – trust me – it really works!

All life is an experiment. The more experiments you make, the better.
            ---**Ralph Waldo Emerson**

CHAPTER SEVEN: How to Create Your Own Audio CD's

Why Audio CD's Work in Getting Referrals

I highly recommend that you create your own audio CD on your specialty area to use as a promotional item. People love listening to CD's while driving. I live in the "information age" and people want and need YOUR INFORMATION! Remember, this is your intellectual property. CD's are easy and inexpensive to create, and will benefit you in the following ways:

Designates you as an "expert"
Promotional item for free giveaway
Educate potential clients
Give value added to current clients
Helps potential clients connect with you
Promotional item for potential referral sources
Sell them over the Internet
Include them with your book or article or workbook
Gift that keeps on giving: people loan it to their friends
Keeps your name & phone # where they can see it. People almost NEVER throw away a CD or MP3 player

Your Simple, Step-by-Step Plan to Create Audio CD's or MP3's

1. Write a report on your subject. One double spaced typed page equals approximately one minute of audio.

2. Record your expert report. Option #1: Record your report onto any audio recorder, then

have it transferred onto CD or MP3 (least expensive but lower quality sound.) Option #2: Record your report at a recording studio (usual charge is $50 - $100 per hour). Your recording person will give you a master CD.

    3. Look in the yellow pages for Audio/Visual Duplicating Companies. Call around for best prices. They can cost you as little as $1.50 each, in quantities of 100 or more. Make sure the company can provide CD covers also – they should have a large selection. Plastic covers like the ones you would buy in a store would run about $3 each. You can also have your audio duplicated on MP3 and these tiny devices have an ethernet adapter for use on any computer. Also, make sure they can put text and graphics onto your CD's and covers.

    4. Take (or mail) your master CD to the company you have chosen, along with a disk of your name, address, phone #, logo, graphics and title of your CD. If you do not have a logo or graphics that is fine. They can create graphics for you or just keep to simple text. Remember, fluff and fancy is not your goal. Your goal is to get them made and into the hands of potential clients and referral sources!

    5. Copyright your CD. <u>Option #1</u>: Copyright it yourself by simply printing onto the CD the symbol © with the year it was produced. This option is legal but does not hold as much validity in court as option #2. <u>Option #2</u>: Have the U.S. Copyrights Office copyright it (Library of Congress). Go to the website www.copyright.gov and they will give you instructions. This costs only about $25 but takes 6 months to a year to receive it. While you are waiting you can still use your own copyright.

    6. Proof your text/copy that will go onto your CD and covers.

    7. Order a small quantity at first until you are sure you will need more. Do not be talked into huge quantities for a lower price. Just have the number

made that you will use in the next few months. You can always order more at any time, or make changes in your text/copy.

Now, once you have your CD's, start giving them out to potential client and referral sources! Offer them as a free giveaway if someone calls in response to your ad (this way you find out if anyone actually read your ad!). Give one to the local library for people to check out. Sell them if you want. Mail them to all your referral sources and potential referral sources. Mail them to former clients as a way to keep in touch and reactivate some of them. Give them to your current clients. This is your VOICE. This is your GIFT. This is a way you can help many more people and promote yourself at the same time!!!

In all realms of life, it takes courage to stretch your limits, express your power, and fulfill your potential; it's no different in the financial realm.
---Suze Orman

CHAPTER EIGHT:
How to Get Referral Sources to Keep Sending You More

Exact Guidelines for How to Thank Your Referrers

The best way to ensure that a first time referrer will continue to refer is to send them a thank you note. A sample "Thank You Letter" is included here. I cannot ethically or legally pay for referrals, or barter for referrals. Therefore, it is best not to try to "repay" your referrer. Merely acknowledging the referrer for the referral is an excellent way to keep them coming. Make sure, however, before you thank the referral source, you ask for permission from your client to thank the referrer. Otherwise, it is a breach of confidentiality. And if the referrer asks for any information about the client, be sure you tell him/her that you are unable to discuss the case any further than this, because of confidentiality laws. If the referrer would like feedback (i.e., another healthcare provider, physician, etc.) about the client's progress, you must get the client's written permission. This is an issue you and your client need to discuss regarding the appropriateness of information exchange.

Gratitude and the Law of Attraction

The movie *"The Secret"* is about how thoughts become things and I create/manifest through our thoughts/visualizations and intentions. One of the main premises of the movie was that *gratefulness* is one of the keys to manifesting what I want. I have always believed in this concept, and have made it a daily practice to write and state grateful affirmations. I give thanks in advance for all that I desire, and give thanks after I receive it. This premise also works in getting more of what I want. People love to hear the words "thank you." Thanking your referral sources both in advance and after sending you referrals <u>will ensure you keep getting more</u>.

What to Send at the Holiday Seasons to Make Your Referrals Skyrocket

Here's your number one, BEST PRACTICE PROMOTION. Send thank you notes or gifts to all your referral sources and potential referral sources at holiday seasons. A little gratitude goes a long way. It is commonplace in the business world to give gifts, buy lunches or dinners, etc., to good referral sources. I have to be very careful in our business not to break ethical or legal standards. Perhaps this is why so few healthcare providers give gifts, lunches, cards, anything to their referral sources. They are so fearful it will look like a payback. But I can implement some of these practices. You need to use your best judgment on this.

I recommend you <u>never give clients gifts</u> (other than your information that is relevant to their health). Birthday and holiday cards with a simple, professional note are fine in most cases. Here, I are discussing referral sources other than clients. Certainly, do not include a gift, or gift offer, in your thank you note for a specific referral. At some <u>other</u> time, call and ask them to lunch (standard practice). Holiday gifts are also pretty standard and traditional in the business world. Gift ideas include candy, flowers, tickets to a sporting event, theater or movies, gift certificates for restaurants or entertainment, food baskets, etc. Never, I repeat <u>never</u>, send wine, champagne, or alcohol of any kind. Keep it clean, healthy, and light.

I think Thanksgiving is the best holiday to send gifts, because it is a time to celebrate what I are grateful for, a non-denominational holiday, and your gift will stand out much more than any other time. Other holidays work Ill also, such as New Years, Valentines Day, Easter/Passover, and 4th of July. I encourage you to send a card or letter to each and every referral source – both those who have referred clients to you in the past and those whom you HOPE will send referrals to you in the future – thanking them. This is a very effective way to build positive relationships, do some networking, keep your name in the forefront of their minds, and create good will. The "law of reciprocity" states that when you give someone something it compels them to want to give you something in return. It's okay to encourage your referral sources to send you referrals this way – it really works!

The 3 BEST Ways to Thank Referral Sources

There are basically three different things you can do, depending on your resources and drive.

1. Do it the old-fashioned way. Send a thank you card. Use your own handwriting on the envelope and inside. Keep your thank you "generic," i.e. "thank you for your referrals this past year," or "thank you for sending me clients you think could benefit from my services." Be sure to include several of your business cards and mention your "offer" or provide a stack of "offer coupons" (see sample below). Your "offer" is something of value that is FREE to them (and the clients they refer to you), such as a 30 minute telephone consultation or your free expert report.

2. Send a thank you letter printed on your letterhead, in your letterhead envelope (see sample below). This way you can include your flyers or brochures along with your letter. You can also send

your FREE promotional item, such as your CD or information booklets.

      3. Send a gift with a thank you card. Keep your gifts simple, not elaborate. Ideas are: box of cookies or candy, fruit basket, case of poIr bars, case of Dannon Light & Fit Smoothies, etc. Address the gift to the professional "and staff." Remember, the staff often is in a better position to refer clients than the professional is. Also, the staff may have treatment needs themselves. Take time to create a positive relationship with the whole office or organization if you can. One woman at my seminar said she recently sent physicians a red box of candy with a gold bow, in a red mailing envelope, with a red thank you card, and her business cards which had red lettering on them. She got tons of thanks and appreciation (and a few client referrals too!).

      As you can see, it is relatively inexpensive and easy to get many good referral sources. It is the <u>MOST COST EFFECTIVE</u> and <u>PROFESSIONAL</u> way to build your practice. Get started <u>today</u>, on your step-by-step plan to win over new referral sources. It's worth it.

I bless others' good fortune, and I know that there's plenty for all. I know that my consciousness determines my prosperity, so I say "yes" to all good. I can rejoice out loud when I see abundance, and mentally make room for it to come into our lives. Being grateful for what you have helps to increase it.
      ---**Louise Hay**

A Simple Letter, Sent to the Right People, Done the Right Way
Will Swamp You With New, Good Business

Sample Thank You Letter

Dear Colleague, Professional, Friend:

It's Thanksgiving, and I'd like to take the time to show my gratitude for referring clients to me. I really appreciate it!

My best referrals are those that come by word of mouth, especially from another trusted professional. It is people like you who help me build a successful practice.

I am expanding my practice to accommodate Saturday morning "intensive couples treatment." These sessions are two to four hours in length. Clients have asked for this type of service and I'm happy to provide it.

Feel free to call me if you have any questions.
With Gratitude,
Lyn Kelley, Ph.D., LMFT, CPC
858-484-8706

Sample Coupon that Compels People to Call You

Lyn Kelley, Ph.D., CPC
Certified Professional Coach

I offer telephone and email coaching
Together I can determine if I can assist you with your goals!
growpublications@yahoo.com

CHAPTER NINE:
Why You Should Accept Credit and Debit Cards

Benefits of Hiring a Billing Service

I encourage you to <u>hire a billing service</u>! As you know, I'm a big fan of "fee-for-service" and "getting paid at the time of service." And of course, I encourage you stay away from managed care and not accept assignment of benefits with insurance companies. So why then, would I promote your use of a billing service? **Here's why**.

Whether you are a coach or a therapist, your goal is to get paid **your full fee**. Fee-for-service clients generally want to pay with debit cards, credit cards or at the end of each month from an invoice. Often they do not even bring their checkbook or credit card with them to your office. Even if they are only paying a small co-pay, they will want to give you their credit/debit card. They can give you the number and expiration date once, and you never have to ask them for it again – if it expires, simply as the client to provide you with a new card or expiration date.

Never Bill Out Again!
The 1-2-3 System that Gets 99% of Clients to Pay You at the Time of Service

Often your sessions are by telephone. **You need to spend your entire session focusing on their treatment, not on collecting money**. You need to spend your time and energy doing what you do best – providing quality care to your clients, and promoting yourself to new, potential clients. You should not be doing paperwork at all (other than writing reports you're getting <u>paid</u> for)! <u>You should not have to worry about the money</u>. Plus, accepting credit cards makes you appear more like a legitimate business.

Some providers feel there is an ethical issue about accepting credit cards, as they fear they would be enabling their clients to build and/or maintain debt. This depends on your client's circumstance. Most people nowadays prefer using credit cards and debit cards to cash or checks. Most affluent people use credit/debit cards for all their purchases. Many people pay off their credit cards at the end of each month, or when they receive their holiday bonus or income tax refund. Many people use their cards against a home equity line of credit. Many people want to earn frequent flyer points by using a certain card. Many people find it advantageous to use credit cards. Find out what works best for your client.

The 1-2-3 system is easy as pie. First you get the client to fill out an authorization form, authorizing you to bill their credit/debit card only for sessions used (and no-shows). Then you get their credit/debit card number, expiration date and billing address. Then you simply input this information into your online merchant account or give to your billing person. Your money should be transferred into your business checking account within 48 hours. Badabing!

Get Rid of Your Collection Accounts!
(It's actually quite easy to get paid when you have experts working for you)

I'm a big fan of hiring experts. I want to focus on my expertise, and allow others to assist me in areas I do not care for or do not have expertise in. I learned this from watching successful business people. The most successful entrepreneurs are rarely afraid to let go of control and allow others to work for them.

I'd like to recommend that you hire a billing service to process your credit cards and do your insurance billing for you. They can usually get a less expensive rate as they work in bulk, and it prevents you from having to take the time to fill out lengthy applications or purchase expensive software or telephone equipment. Here are some of the other benefits to you:

Saves you TONS of time
Saves you paperwork hassles
Frees you up to focus on client/patient care
Sets up your credit card system for you so the $$ goes directly into your checking account
Allows you to accept electronic checks
Allows you to charge your full fee (and collect it!)
Sets up client/patient payment plans
Tracks client/patient payments for you
Provides management support to you
Easier to charge for no-shows
Easier to charge for extra phone consults or emergency phone exchanges
Allows you to get collection issues off your plate
Frees you up to spend the entire session focusing on your clients
No wasting time going to the bank to deposit paper checks
No more worrying client might "forget their checkbook"

5 Ways to Turn Your Website Into a Sales Machine

Step One: Build an effective shopping cart. Some small businesses use services such as PayPal for making and receiving online payments. I recommend using PayPal at first, and later work on building a full-featured shopping cart directly into your website. Shopping carts allow for more customization and the potential to provide more product information.

I recommend PayPal, as it is the most well-known way of sending and receiving money, and your clients trust it. There are many other payment apps such as Venmo, Zelle, Google Pay, and Square. These are also very popular and trusted. When I do consultations, I ask my clients to pay me FIRST. I can either send them an invoice to pay from or they can just send me money through whatever app they prefer.

There are many shopping cart software programs available, and sifting through them can take quite a bit of time. *Volusion* is an all-in-one shopping-cart tool that starts at $19 per month and handles checkout and payment processing. It offers more than 120 customizable online store templates that are smartphone and tablet-friendly. You also can showcase product options, add unlimited photos and make product comparisons. *BigCommerce*, another shopping-cart software provider, offers a similar package starting at about $25 per month. It includes customizable designs and can be integrated with social media and third-party services such as *Google Product Search.*

Step Two: Recommend related products. Amazon.com has paved the way with their add-on sales pages. Every time you search for a product on Amazon, you can scroll down the page and see "Shoppers Who Viewed This Product Also Viewed These." They give you a few more options to compare your item with, and/or items that may go nicely with the item you're interested in. An online store can include a "recommendation engine" that suggests complementary products, upgrades and additional services. For example, if a customer puts a grill in his online shopping cart, he can be prompted to also consider buying tongs and a spatula.

Step Three: Optimize your site for search engines. A website can't sell if it can't be found. So, follow all my advice for SEO above.

Step Four: Start a contest or promotion. An online contest or promotion can help attract attention in social media channels and lure potential customers to your site. Giving away a high value item can stir up the most attention but frequent, simple contests with smaller perks can also be effective. There are many software programs that offer web-based contest platforms for a reasonable price. They can make it easier to organize and run promotions such as simple giveaways, coupons and sweepstakes. They manage the basics of asking visitors to like your page, fill out a form or join an email list.

Step Five: Develop a shipping strategy. When it comes to e-commerce, free or steeply discounted shipping is quickly becoming the standard. But to compete with big online retailers, you'll need to ship strategically. Instead of opting for either costly or completely free shipping, you might consider something in between. You could make only ground shipping free and set a minimum purchase amount to qualify. Personally, I use USPS and ship most of my packages "priority mail." I charge $10 - $30 for shipping and handling charges. I also have USPS computer software program that prints my shipping labels and postage marks for me called www.Stamps.com. This makes things much easier for me. Most of my packages are small enough to place outside near my mailbox and the regular mail carrier will pick them up. If I had a lot of packages to ship daily I would use one of the larger mailing companies such as UPS, since they will pick up for free.

Every calling is great when greatly pursued.
---Oliver Wendell Holmes, Jr.

You don't serve yourself or the world by playing small.
---Marianne Williamson

CHAPTER 10:
10 Simple Things You Need to Do Right Now

1. Give clients options of how to pay (Credit Card, Debit Card, Automatic Checks, etc.).

2. Raise your fees 10% for all new clients. Do not accept any new clients who cannot pay your full fee.

3. Allow only 10 – 15% of your practice for no fee, low fee.

4. Save your most coveted hours (PM's, evenings, weekends) for FULL-PAYING CLIENTS.

5 Phase out of managed care. Determine which managed care plan is the lowest paying, most difficult – then fire them! This will create the space you need for new, Ill-paying clients.

6. Start sending out a monthly or bi-monthly newsletter.

7. Develop a new niche that is positive and will attract a higher paying, higher functioning clientele. Write an article about it or record an audio CD on it to use as a promotional item.

8. Reactivate former clients (or get them to remember to refer people to you). A former client will return to you if they want/need to, right? Wrong! Studies show that 68% of your clients WANT to return, but DON'T, until you do THIS. Send them an invitation! Type up a "reactivation letter" on your letterhead. Pull together all names

and addresses of current and former clients and put them into a data base or have a mailing house do it for you. Mail these letters out NOW.

9. Give something away free.

10. Write your free offer on your business cards and tell it to anyone and everyone. Give your business cards to every business person/professional you come into contact with.

Do all these things in the next 3 months to get yourself into position to have an even better year! Make it your goal to work less, earn more, and enjoy your life more this year! Watch your practice bloom!

Everything is perfect in the universe – even your desire to improve it.
---Wayne Dyer

Chapter 11
The Most Effective Marketing Strategies
(which are not marketing!)

How to Target and Promote SPECIFICALLY to a Well-Pay, Self-Pay Clientele

In his book, *Guerrilla Marketing*, Jay Conrad Levinson explains that effective marketing is a combination of strategy and tactics that enable you to market products and services with imagination and energy rather than the brute force of a huge budget. The essence of Guerrilla Marketing can be understood in just seven words -- each ending in the letters "ent" (which are the last 3 letters in the word "intent"):

Assortment: The greater variety of your marketing vehicles, the more effective.
Commitment: Market with a clear and simple plan to which you can commit and stick with.
Investment: Marketing expenditures are an investment in your business. Invest in what you believe in.
Consistent: People want to do business with people who are solid. Build up a sense of stability and security through familiarity in your marketing techniques.
Confident: Make sure you promote yourself confidently. A nationwide study showed this to be the single most powerful influence over sales. Second was quality, third was service, and 4th was selection.
Patient: Give your marketing plan time to work. Remember, you are investing in the building of your business.

Subsequent: Continue marketing to your current and former customers -- they will bring you repeat and referral business. Develop new products and services. Don't stop at getting new customers. Studies show that 80% of business that is lost is due to apathy after the sale.

How to Get People to KNOW-LIKE-TRUST You

Here is where people get to KNOW-LIKE-TRUST you. When you meet them face to face. You put yourself out there. You meet and greet. You get to know people on a personal level. You give them your business card and mission statement and they either make an appointment for themselves or refer someone to you.

1. Public and Corporate Seminars -- By conducting seminars, you not only credential yourself in the community as an expert, educate people on mental Illness, but you make yourself attractive as a provider. You get your name and face out to clients who would not otherwise know about you. You begin to develop a trusting relationship with potential clients. When word gets out that you are an expert and that you give talks, you will eventually be hired for these services as Ill as your healthcare services.

You need to create a flyer or brochure on the topics you feel qualified to discuss. This will assist you in developing and refining your therapeutic niche or specialty. Once you have decided on several topics and have created a flyer with an outline on each, you are ready to contact agencies and corporations in your community with an offer to present a short (30 — 60 minute) seminar or talk to their members. You can get a listing of business in your zip code area from your local library. You might want to obtain a directory and mail them a letter with your brochure or flyers. You will address these letters to the Human Resources Representative of the corporation, or the Director of the agency or organization. Professional organizations, such as the Lions Club, Rotary Club, Chamber of Commerce, are a good place to start. Then work on mental health agencies such as the Red Cross, United Way, Psychiatric Hospitals, etc.

I believe the richest pool of potential good clients is the corporations. This is because 1) they have the largest number of employees, 2) they usually have an in-house Illness program that they already have scheduled for their employees, 3) they are very interested in giving their employees good Illness advice (most corporations receive significant discounts on their health insurance premiums if they offer their own Illness Program), 4) working employees make good clients because they are usually responsible, hold a good job, and can pay your fee. You can offer a free talk during their lunch hour that is voluntary to them.

Obtain a listing of local corporations from your local library or Chamber of Commerce. The agency or business you are presenting to will usually offer to advertise your talk for you. They will even create flyers and post them, or place them in employee's mailboxes. All you have to do is show up. Your presentation does not have to be extremely polished. You can bring some notes, talk for 15 or 20 minutes, and then allow time for questions and answers and discussion. You will hand out your business cards and any other free gift you have, i.e., audio tapes, articles, etc. This is how I started my practice and it was a great way to get new clients fairly quickly.

If the Human Resources Representative likes you, you can offer to come back and do a series. Now you will be developing even more of a trusting relationship with a rich pool of potential clients.

Also, it is a great way to become a provider for their EAP program, or even their Managed Care Programs if you desire. A word of caution here — do not offer to reduce your fee for any of their in house or insurance counseling programs. You will be getting so many new clients on your own that you do not have to "sell out" to them in exchange for their referrals.

The best thing about giving presentations is that it doesn't cost you anything but your time. Spending a few hours a month on this will pay off tremendously. As a by-product, you may find that you enjoy it and you will receive validation and reinforcement for your work. People really appreciate a good presentation, as they know how difficult it is to speak in front of people.

2. In-House Seminars/Time-limited Groups -- This idea is essentially the same as the one stated above, except that it is conducted at your office site. The advantage to this is that attendees will see your office, become familiar with the location, and get a feel for what it would be like to come for counseling. The disadvantage is that you will have to do your own advertising. The best way to advertise your seminars is through display ads in local newspapers and in the "Calendar" section of these papers. A "Calendar" or "Bulletin Board" ad is usually free, but doesn't pull the response that a display ad does. A good display ad must be at least 2" x 3", and preferably will have a picture of you on it with a caption. Depending on how often you run it, the cost will be $150 to $300 per ad.

I recommend you create an in-house "Wellness Program" and make a flyer with the topics and dates for the year. This way you can send it to your local newspapers, give it to current clients, mail it to former clients, and post it around town. I recommend you charge a nominal fee, approximately

$5 or $10, just enough to cover the cost of your advertising and refreshments. Saturday mornings and mid-Week evenings are the best times to offer them. I always include coffee and a snack because psychologically people equate food with warmth, caring, and sharing.

Even if you dislike speaking, you can keep your talk casual and light, short and sweet. Adults tend to prefer discussion and activity anyway. State a few main points, then have them complete an exercise that will get them thinking and discovering something new. Keep the entire class to about one to one and a half hour. This gives them just enough new information to feel they've received some value and not so much that they get bored and restless.

You could even show your video tape at the seminar and offer discussion around it. If you have created a "free gift," give it to them when they leave with your business card. Make sure they leave with something in their hands that they will use, read, or listen to at home. This will keep memory fresh in their minds, and be a constant reminder to them that you are there. I once had a client call me for an appointment who said she had carried my business card in her wallet for three years! This investment will pay off for you in the short and long run.

Time-limited groups are a great idea if you want more self-pay clients. In a report by Psychotherapy Finances (Jan. 1998), a therapist who has found success with anxiety groups is highlighted. According to this article, there are many advantages to having a group therapy program. First, potential clients who are "put off" by the idea of "psychotherapy" may be less resistant to group therapy, educational or support groups. Also, it is more affordable than individual therapy, and can bolster your out-of-pocket business. And it's a more efficient use of your time. Six patients paying a lower fee will still net you more income than one individual session. And six patients can provide you with a lot more referrals.

     3. Be on the Advisory Board of a Company -- Many large companies are looking for ways to decrease their health insurance premiums, and the one way to do that is too keep their employees healthy and have low medical claims. This way, the next year when they re-negotiate their health insurance contracts, the premiums will go down. You could offer to be on a committee or board when you meet the Human Resources Director at the corporations you give talks to.
     Being part of a board is a great way to get your name out and it is a very low key, inexpensive promotion that generates new clients in a dignified manner.

     4. Set Up a Booth at Health Fairs -- Having a booth at a fair or festival is not only a lot of fun, but it serves to generate new referrals. There are several types of health fairs that offer booths for you to promote your practice. One is large corporations often have annual health fairs in house. The best way to find out about company health fairs is to call the Human Resources Department of large corporations and ask them if they are planning anything like this and ask how you can become a part of it.
     Another type is at a Community Festival or Health Fair that offers a business or trade section as part of their fair. This is a great way to get to know people in your community. I do not recommend having a booth at a Business Trade Show because the attendees will be mainly other professionals like you looking for new business ideas and resources. You need to focus your efforts on booths where there will be a high volume of people who may want your services. The general public and employees of large

corporations are your best sources of potential clients.

New age/holistic health types of fairs or shows are an excellent source of interested potential clients. You will need to always give something free. Keep in mind that it must be something of value, and something they will keep. A great idea is a refrigerator magnet with a listing of local emergency phone numbers, and of course, your name, address, and phone number. Again, this is a place you will want to have educational materials on display. I had tape recorders and biofeedback temperature cards so they could listen and get a quick lesson in biofeedback and keep their temperature card. People loved this, especially children. You may even find, as I did, that people would like to purchase your books, tapes, or pamphlets.

I co-rented the booth with another mental health provider to help share costs and have someone to talk to when traffic was slow. One partner brought her tapes on hypnosis and allowed people to listen to segments of her "Stop Smoking," "weight Control," and "Athletic Performance Enhancement" tapes. Her three headsets Ire being used all day, with people waiting in line. If only she'd had some there for sale, she could have paid back the booth rental (about $100) and earned some money as Ill. It turned out that she had more appointments than she could handle the following Week. She had three new clients come in the very next day.

5. Radio and TV Talk Shows -- This is a favorite of mine and it is very simple. All you do is send a proposal to the local radio and TV stations in your community and offer to do the show from their office or from your own office via telephone. You can give the talk show host a list of good questions on the topic and you can discuss these questions with the host. Typically, people call in and you give

advice and answer questions. Again, you are presenting yourself as an expert and getting your word and name out. You can record the show, write up a transcript of it, or make a CD of it for your "free gift."

6. Teach Courses for Adult Education -- In many cities there is an organization called "The Learning Annex" that publishes and sponsors seminars on various different topics of local public interest. They charge anywhere from $24 to $150 per seminar. They pay their seminar leaders a percentage of the fees brought in. This is a great way to get publicity and make a little extra money on the side. Teaching courses for a respected organization, i.e., the local community college or adult education program will be fun and give you credibility and visibility. The organization that sponsors you will be advertising and promoting you at their expense -- not yours.

7. Join a Speakers Bureau -- There are national and local speakers associations in almost every major city. Membership fees range from $50 to $500, depending on the chapter and type of membership. Once you are a member, and provide the association with a profile sheet and speaking proposals, they will list you in their speakers listing and advertise for you on the Internet, through direct mail, and other means of marketing. The great thing about these organizations is that they can give you assistance in giving presentations, receive excellent training, and they can promote you. You also get paid for your services at a higher rate by joining an association. The local chapter of my professional association has its own speaker's bureau, which is free for members. I received at least three requests per month to speak for various organizations when I was active. You must pick and choose your

audience, however, and make sure they are local and are in your target market.

Remember earlier I talked about knowing the value of a satisfied client? The most important thing to know is the total value of each satisfied patient is at least $3,840 if your average fee is $80 and the clients come an average of 12 sessions. Now think about that... $3,840 is the value of each satisfied patient. If I said it would cost you $1,000 to get a new client and it would cost you $10,000 for 10 new clients, you'd probably say, "that's crazy! I don't want to spend that kind of money. It would never be worth it." But think about it. Those 10 clients would be worth a total of $38,400 for a total cost of $10,000. In other words, you'd be getting back $3.84 for each dollar spent. Most of the strategies in this book will give you a better return than this and cost you much less up front.

So when you consider smart marketing ideas that might cost $300, you should see a return on investment of $3,000. Try to remember that even though it may seem like a lot of money to put up front, good, well planned marketing efforts do pay off. You should get back at least $3.84 for each advertising dollar that you spend, or the ad/promotion probably wasn't very effective. You need to find out which of the ideas presented in this course do pay off for you. You may be earning 100 times your ad expenses with some of our ideas. Not only that, you'll be having a good time while building a good practice reputation in the community.

How to Obtain Your GOLDMINE List – Your High Yield Target Market

Your mailing list will be your GOLDMINE to your success. You will want to obtain email and mailing addresses from as many people as possible.

This way you can stay in touch with them on a regular basis. You can purchase mailing addresses from a list broker, but you cannot purchase email addresses, so email addresses are much more coveted. Collect contact information from friends, family, acquaintances, current clients, former clients, potential referral sources and current referral sources. Create a database and make sure you back it up monthly so you never lose these important contacts!

"A dream not followed by consistent action, however humble or small the actions may be, points to either a huge contradiction or a gigantic misunderstanding. Because when people get clear and realize just how powerful they truly are, wild horses can't stop them from taking even the humblest of baby steps, every day."
----Mike Dooley

CHAPTER 12:
Integrating Social Media

The FREE Online Promotion that Makes You a Celebrity

Social media has become the number one source for online referrals for most entrepreneurs. Even if you don't want to play the social media game, it's the new game in town, and if you want more referrals you're going to have to be a player. Whether you like it or not, you're going to need to promote yourself and your business through this venue. It's virtually FREE for you, and it can be very effective, if you know how to play the game the right way. The way I tell you!

Okay, so you've heard you need to get your business and name KNOWN. People are telling you that you need to get on social media networking for your business. People are talking all about Facebook, MySpace, Twitter, etc. You've heard that you need to get an audience of "fans" from all over the world to promote your business. You want to become a celebrity in your field. You've heard that it's basically a free way to promote yourself, and it's easy to do. You've heard you can sell your products this way, too. That's all true and good, but...

You also know that most of these sites are used primarily for "social" use, not business use. You want to look professional, and aren't sure if these sites will make you look like you're just trying to make friends and build a fan base. You aren't sure which sites would be the best for your type of practice. You aren't sure how to do it, or what to do on a daily basis. You aren't sure how much time it will involve. You're stuck in indecision.

Well, I'm here to help you make some sense of it and make it easier for you! With millions of people using these sites on a daily basis, social networking platforms have become a virtual window to FREE internet promotion, reaching millions of people all over the world on a daily basis. This type of promotion is generally for social connections with people who share your interests. This is great except that you are not about SOCIAL networking. You are about BUSINESS networking.

This being said, you can and should get a fan base on as many social media sites as you can. It really depends on your business, which sites and how many sites to be on. Taco Bell and Pizza Hut have been very successful at it, since they are constantly giving people online coupons and free offers. Many businesses offer special deals and perks if you "like" their page. The BEST way of advertising is WORD OF MOUTH. Your social media "followers" and "friends" will tell their other followers and friends about you, and this is a great way to build your business.

LinkedIn is the largest and most popular business networking site, and it has proven to be very effective and professional. Face-book and Twitter are the two most popular social sites at the time of this writing, but as you know, in the online world, things change at the speed of light. Follow the same basic rules I already gave you for your website, for your social media advertising.

7 Essential Rules for Building a Loyal Customer from Social Media Networking

Social Media Networking has completely changed the way we do business and the way we connect, build, and maintain our relationships on both a personal and professional basis. If you haven't already jumped on the Social Media bandwagon, now would be the time! Social Media started out as a way of connecting with friends and colleagues, and has now become the fastest growing method of professional marketing in the world. Since it's completely FREE to you, and takes very little time, and is fun to do, there's no good excuse to not implement this powerful strategy!

Face-book (FB), which was launched just six years ago, is the most popular Social Media site, leading all the others in popularity. FB seems to stay one step ahead of its competition such as Twitter, LinkedIn, MySpace, YouTube and Google. Mark Zuckerberg's mission statement for FB is, "To give people the power to share, and help make the world more open and connected such that world problems might be solved." That is one B.H.A.G. (big, hairy audacious goal)!

For the purposes of this book, I will assume you have (or will soon have) a professional site for at least three of the above named social media sites. I use my personal name for all of them, but I mainly use them for business purposes. It took me a few years to get over 800 "friends" on FB, and I keep adding to my list daily, although I am selective. It took me a year to get 200 Twitter "followers," as this is NOT an easy process! My FB, Twitter and LinkedIn accounts are linked so when I post something on one site, it automatically posts it to the other two sites (saves time).

Here are your 7 essential rules for making Social Media work for your business:

Essential Rule #1: Be Yourself

Be authentic, positive and connecting. Spend some time each day "liking" other people's posts and/or making validating comments on them. Always keep your posts positive. Try to avoid political statements, religious statements, opinions and judgments. You don't want to turn people away. Just be your best, most genuine, positive self and people will move toward you like a plant moves toward the sun.

Essential Rule #2: Keep Your Privacy and Be Selective

You should always be yourself, however, this doesn't mean you need to be completely OPEN. Be very careful about how much personal information you post or the types of photos you post. Every time I post something, before I click "post" I ask myself, "How would my customers view this?" I want to be myself, yet I want to maintain my professional integrity. I feel it's okay for my professional customers to see that I am a real person, with a family, friends, social activities and interests. I try to be myself, yet somewhat reserved.

All the Social Media sites have privacy settings. I keep everything to only my "friends." Whenever a new person asks to join my network, I look at their site and read a bit about them before "accepting" them. I try to screen out people who I think would have no interest in my services. Many people use Social Media to make friends, find mates, get dates, or other reasons that are not of interest to you as a professional. If you find you've "accepted" a friend or follower who turns out to be negative in any way, you can "hide" them or "un-friend" them without them even knowing. My rule is, if they rub me the wrong way (I feel a crunch in my gut) they're OUT.

Essential Rule #3: Make Sure People Know What You Offer

We live in an attention-based world now more than ever and people often just have a <u>nanosecond</u> to see your site and decide whether you're a fit for their network or not. For this reason, it's important to display total CLARITY in what you do, who you help, and how you help. Make sure they can see right away what you do – make it easy for people to get to know you and do business with you.

Be careful not to overdo the links on your profile page. I recommend just showing your website and/or blog, along with a link to your other social media sites as appropriate. On your FB personal profile page and on your fan page, there is a small field under your photo where you can write your mission statement or "tag line."

Essential Rule #4: Be Generous and Have an Abundance Mindset

I truly believe there's enough for everyone and there's no such thing as competition, particularly in a service-based business. Show your generosity by giving your connections something free – and offer it on a regular basis – changing it every month or so. For example, in February you can give ½ hour free telephone relationship advice, in March you can give your free booklet or article on "Financial Stress," and in April you can give a free book (either one you've written or one you love) to the first 12 people who ask. Remember, the favorite word in the English language is FREE!

Essential Rule #5: To be an Authority You Need to be an Author, Writer and/or Publisher

Author Gary Vaynerchuk talks about how every business should get into the "content business." This means you need to write about your specialties and expertise. You can write articles, pamphlets, e-books, and blog posts. If you're passionate about your topic you'll never run out of content. FB gives you an opportunity to publish a wide variety of content types, from photos, videos, links, notes, comments, articles, and more. By regularly posting (ideally once per day at a minimum), you can deliberately manage how you are perceived among your network. Everything you post should be with strategic intent. The more content you produce, the more authority and credibility you will command. By giving your best stuff away for free your connections will think that if you're this knowledgeable and generous with your free stuff, your paid stuff must be really fabulous!

Essential Rule #6: Connect with People

As important as "content" is, I believe "connection" is better. In other words, I put relationships first, business second. As Suzie Orman says, "Relationships first, then money, then things." One of the main reasons new customers give for calling ME as opposed to all the OTHERS is that they felt I was more approachable. They could tell by the way I present myself on my social media sites, my YouTube videos, my audiobooks, my e-books and my website, that I would be someone who would understand them and help them. I spend about 15 minutes a day responding to other people's posts, "liking" them, "sharing" them, and "re-tweeting" them. I send responses to people who I don't know, who NEVER write to me or respond to me. That's okay. When they see my posts enough times, they will at some point either pay attention or remember me through <u>repetition and visibility</u>.

Essential Rule #7: Have an Objective Strategy and Means of Measurement

Let's say your initial objective is to get your first 1000 fans. Even then, you need to have a sub-objective as to what you want those fans to DO. Perhaps you're simply building community for now, so you want the fans to keep coming back and interacting. Or maybe you want them to opt in to your email list to access a free give or monthly newsletter. Maybe you want them to call you for an appointment. Maybe you want them to sign up for your "program." Either way, be sure to measure your progress.

Strategies for adding fans could be broadcasting to your existing email list, writing blog posts, and signing every email with your request to "Follow Me" with a link to all your sites. By the way, be sure you have links on the homepage of your website for people to follow you!

Take imperfect action and be patient. It's not realistic to expect you'll have a ton of fans right away. You are investing in the long-term success of your business. Do at least one thing every day toward it. Investing your time now, will pay dividends later.

Social Networking Do's and Don'ts

Here are some tips and instructions for you if you do decide to do social networking and promoting.

DO: Register on as many websites as you think would promote you. To effectively use social media techniques to promote your business, you can't rely on just one network. Register with numerous sites, such as Face-book, Twitter and LinkedIn, and complete your online profile for each site you join.

DO: Decide what type of associates you're going to target and connect with them. Most sites allow you to browse user profiles and send friend requests. Browse for people and groups who have listed interests that relate to your business and add them to your network. Once you have accumulated these friends, you can interact with tem within the network publicly and/or via private messages.

DO: Interact with your network on a personal level. Though you are using social media sites for business, remember that overdoing it can make your profile lean more toward an advertisement than a social networking profile. Mention your business, products or services, but don't be overly self-promotional. Speak to your audience on a casual level about topics relevant to your business.

DO: Add your website link to each article, blog, bulletin or event invitation. You can link to any page you want that is relevant to the topic of your post. This technique can drive more traffic to your site.

DO: Link your social networking profiles. If you're promoting your business on multiple websites, let your audience know that. For example, include a link to your Twitter page on your Face-book page. To save time and reach more people, connect all of your social media accounts to post items, like bulletins, blogs and press releases – to all of your profiles at once.

DO: Keep your social media profiles active and current. The most effective way to use your social media profiles to promote your business is to remain active. Post items on a regular, frequent basis – at least once a week. Making your presence known will draw attention from other users and maintain a constant flow of fresh content to attract search engine attention and increase your page ranking. Social media sites use ranking similar to the way the large search engines (such as Google, Yahoo, MSN) do.

DON'T: Overdo it. Repetitive links, comments, emails and blog posts are considered spam on most websites and may result in suspension or removal of your company profile.

Far better is it to dare mighty things, to win glorious triumphs, even though checkered by failure than to rank with those poor spirits who neither enjoy nor suffer much, because they live in a gray twilight that knows not victory nor defeat.
---Theodore Roosevelt

CHAPTER 13:
Dramatic No-Cost Results from YouTube

      Another great FREE place to promote your business is on *YouTube*. In fact, I think this is a <u>far more effective promotional strategy</u> than social networking – at least at this point in time. As of right now, it is FREE to post a video clip on YouTube, and it's a great way to advertise your business online. Your video only needs to be a few minutes long, and "how to" instructional videos are best. As I've told you all along, people need to "Know-Like-Trust" you. They can get to know-like-trust you a LOT MORE from a video like this. If you post a video on YouTube, be sure you provide a link to it from your website and all your blogs and social/business networking sites. The more hits you get, the higher your ranking will be.

      If you think you couldn't do a video at home, from your own video recorder, think again. Look at some of the videos people have on YouTube. You'll see that most of them are very amateurish. There is one I like by a young woman who did it herself, and did a great job. Look at hers as an example: http://www.youtube.com/watch?v=RQzHid59I7c. In case you can't link to it, go on www.YouTube.com and put into the search bar: *12 Mistakes Which Lead To Disempowerment and Misery*. This young woman is not a therapist or certified coach but she sure is smart and presents herself very well on this video. People love to watch videos, and they especially love anything with "mistakes," "stupid," "dummies" and "idiots" in the title. You could easily write up something like, "The 10 Most Common Mistakes People Make in their Kitchen Design."

YouTube gives you complete instructions on how to upload your video to their site. You can edit it on their site prior to publishing it. You can add your name and biographical data as well as your website on the site. You will start getting followers and comments. The more "hits" you get, the more likely you will be chosen to put ads onto your video site. This way you can get paid every time someone clicks on an ad from your video. YouTube's free *analytics tool* helps you understand who is watching your ads and how they are interacting with them.

Check out my YouTube videos. They're homespun – not very professional. I just set up my tripod and video camera and recorded them from my office. It doesn't have to be fancy – just be yourself – people will appreciate it!

The Biggest Mistake Women Make in Dating and Love Relationships

Is He a Commitment Phobic?

How to Stick With Your Diet and Exercise Program

How to Become a Certified Professional Coach

Bad Dick, Good Jane: How Good Girls Get Bad Boys to Behave

> *If one advances confidently in the direction of his dreams, and endeavors to live the life which he has imagined, he will meet with a success unexpected in common hours.*
> ---Henry David Thoreau

BONUS:
7 Ways to Double Your Income Without Advertising or Spending ANY Money

Believe it or not, there are simple things you can do to immediately increase your income dramatically without spending a dime! None of these 7 ideas cost you a thing, nor do they take more than a couple of minutes of your time! Sound too good to be true? NOT! Read on:

1. Charge 20% more for couples and family sessions (MediCal and Medicare already allow for higher fees for couples and families!)

2. Offer 80 minute sessions for couples and families and more difficult cases (increases your income by 50%)

3. Offer Marathon Treatment: Daily or 2 – 3 times a Week sessions until crisis is resolved (increases your income by 100 – 200%)

4. Offer Intensive Treatment: 4 hour sessions on weekends (increases your income by 200 – 300%)

5. Offer In-Home Assessments for families, elderly, handicapped and children – charge 20% more portal to portal (increases your income by 50% or more)

6. Offer telephone sessions (1/4 hour to ½ hour) in between face-to-face sessions (increases your income by 25 – 50%)

7. Raise your fees by at least 10% and charge at least 10% more for evening and weekend appointments.

I wish you the very best in this next year! Please contact me if I can help you build and/or improve your practice! Or if you need practice saying "NO!"

Call me for Practice Building Consultation by Phone
Reasonable fee per 1/2 Hour
growpublications@yahoo.com

---At the moment of commitment, the Universe conspires to assist you.
*---***Barbara Streissand**

###

Discover other titles by Lyn Kelley distributed at www.amazon.com

<u>New Release!</u>
Bad Dick, Good Jane: How Good Girls Get Bad Boys to Behave

<u>Dear Jane Series:</u>
The 12 Biggest Mistakes Women Make in Dating & Love Relationships
How to Turn a Player into a Stayer
How to Cure a Commitment-Phobic
Controlling and Manipulative Men: How to Spot Them and Handle Them

Self-Centered and Narcissistic Men: How to Spot Them and Handle Them
Addicted Men: How to Spot Them and Handle Them
Low Achieving Men - Passives, Wimps, Dreamers:
How to Spot Them and Handle Them
Cheap Men: How to Spot Them and Handle Them
Men who Lie and Cheat: How to Spot Them and Handle Them
Emotionally Unavailable Men: How to Spot Them and Handle Them

<u>Other Books:</u>
How to Stick With Your Diet & Exercise Program
How to Motivate People! The 3 Magic Keys to Unlock Anyone's Hidden Motivation
Therapists: How to Promote Your Practice to a Ill-Pay, Self-Pay Clientele
Healthcare Providers: How to Promote Your Practice to a Ill-Pay, Self-Pay Clientele
How to Motivate Your Clients to Change: Psychological Principles of Motivation
How to Become a Life Coach
How to Become a Corporate/Business Coach
How to Become a Virtual Coach
The 7 Secrets of Highly Successful Therapists
The 7 Self-Sabotages: Why People Sabotage Themselves and How to Stop It
Alternative Income Sources for Therapists
Ethical Issues for Coaches
Practice Angels: How to Build a Full Practice from Good Referral Sources Alone
How to Get a Raise from Managed Care Plans

Get New Clients Now! Top 10 Ways to Attract New, Ill-Pay Clients

Become Your Own Life Coach in 12 Easy Steps

One Day She Woke Up and Decided to Be Brave

She Said She Would Be Rich and They Believed Her

Become a Certified Professional Coach through GROW!

The least expensive, easiest, fastest and most comprehensive Coach Training Program available! All done through Home Study. See more info here: https://www.growpublications.com/cms/pages/127-become-a-certified-coach

Learn more about Dr. Lyn at
www.GrowTrainingInstitute.com

Follow me:
Facebook: http://facebook.com/lyn.kelley1

Twitter:
http://wefollow.com/JanesGoodAdvice

LinkedIn:
http://www.linkedin.com/in/drlynisin

Thank You!

www.ingramcontent.com/pod-product-compliance
Lightning Source LLC
Chambersburg PA
CBHW070208230526
45471CB00002B/876